HOUGHTON MIFFLIN HARCOURT

JOURNEYS

Write-In Reader
Grade 2

Printed in the U.S.A.

ISBN: 978-0-547-25415-9

6789 - 0877 - 17 16 15 14 13 12 11

4500290199   B C D E F

 HOUGHTON MIFFLIN HARCOURT
School Publishers

Contents

✓ **TARGET VOCABULARY**

curly

row

stood

straight

My Friends

1 My friend Lisa has **straight** hair. It is very smooth.

Tell about a friend who has straight hair.

_____

_____

_____

2 My friend Miguel has curls and waves in his hair. He has **curly** hair.

Name a friend who has curly hair.

_____

2

3 Paquita is my friend. We played hide-and-seek. Paquita hid behind a bush. It **stood** six feet tall!

Tell about someone who <u>stood</u> taller than you.

_____

_____

_____

4 Bart and his friends played leap frog. They lined up in a **row**. Then they took turns and jumped.

In what other game can kids line up in a <u>row</u>?

_____

_____

_____

3

Best Friends

by Margaret Maugenest

Mai and Jenny were best friends.
They lived next door to each other.

A tree stood between their homes. It had a **straight** trunk. The top of the tree looked like **curly** green hair.

Stop **Think** **Write**

VOCABULARY

The treetop looks a lot like

_____ green hair.

4

Jenny and Mai wrote notes to each other. They put the notes in a tree. It was their secret hiding place.

It was Jenny's birthday. Mai got Jenny a present. She wrote Jenny a note.

Stop **Think** **Write**

CAUSE AND EFFECT

Mai gets Jenny a present for her

_____ .

5

The note said to come to Mai's house. Mai put a red bow around the note. She put it in the tree. Then she waited.

Jenny did not come. Mai checked the tree. Her note was gone.

SEQUENCE OF EVENTS

Mai puts the note in the tree. What does she do after that?

_____

_____

6

Mai looked at Jenny's house. She saw kids. They lined up in a **row**. They had presents. They went into Jenny's house.

Jenny was having a birthday party! Why didn't she invite Mai?

Stop | Think | Write

VOCABULARY

Who lined up in a <u>row</u>?

_____

_____

_____

7

Mai sat on her swing. She felt mad.

Jenny came. "Why aren't you at my party?" she said.

Mai got off the swing. She **stood** tall. "You didn't invite me!" she said.

SEQUENCE OF EVENTS

Stop | **Think** | **Write**

Mai sits on her swing. Then

_____ **comes.**

"I DID invite you. I put a note
in the tree," said Jenny.

The girls heard a noise. They looked
up. They saw a bird in a nest. The nest
had paper. It had a red bow.

Stop | Think | Write

SEQUENCE OF EVENTS

Jenny and Mai hear a noise and look up. They

see a _____ in a nest.

"That bird took our notes. It took the ribbon. It used them for its nest!" said Mai.

Jenny and Mai still write notes to each other. Now they put their notes in a box. They are still best friends.

Stop Think Write

MAIN IDEAS AND DETAILS

The bird used the notes and ribbon to make its

_____ .

Look Back and Respond

1 Where do Jenny and Mai hide notes to each other?

Hint

For a hint, see page 5.

_____

_____

_____

2 Jenny is having a party. How does Mai feel?

Hint

For a hint, see page 8.

_____

_____

_____

3 The girls see the nest. After that, where do they put notes?

Hint

For a hint, see page 10.

_____

_____

_____

Family Parties

Check the answer.

1 Grandma and Grandpa _____ us each summer. They stay at our house. We have a big party for them.

☐ **drooled**   ☐ **visit**   ☐ **stood**

2 It is my birthday! We have a party. Dad puts a _____ on my head.

☐ **crown**   ☐ **row**   ☐ **cousin**

3 My _____ Kaya had a baby. We gave a party. People brought gifts for the baby.

☐ **crown**   ☐ **piano**   ☐ **cousin**

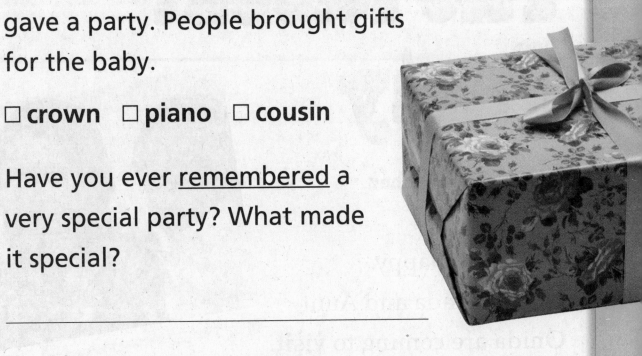

4 Have you ever <u>remembered</u> a very special party? What made it special?

_____

_____

_____

5 Who would you like to <u>visit</u>? Why?

_____

_____

_____

The Nicest Party

by Maria Sánchez

I am so happy.
Uncle Takada and Aunt
Onida are coming to **visit**.
Their daughter, Tala, is coming, too.

I have not met Tala. I've seen pictures.
I like looking at family pictures.

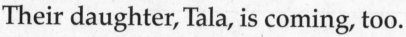

Stop | **Think** | **Write**

Uncle Takada, Aunt Onida, and Tala are coming

to _____.

"We must have a family party!" said Mother.

"May I help?" I asked.

"Yes, Nita," said Mother. "We must shop for party things."

Stop **Think** **Write**

MAIN IDEAS AND DETAILS

What will Nita and her mother buy?

_____

_____

_____

15

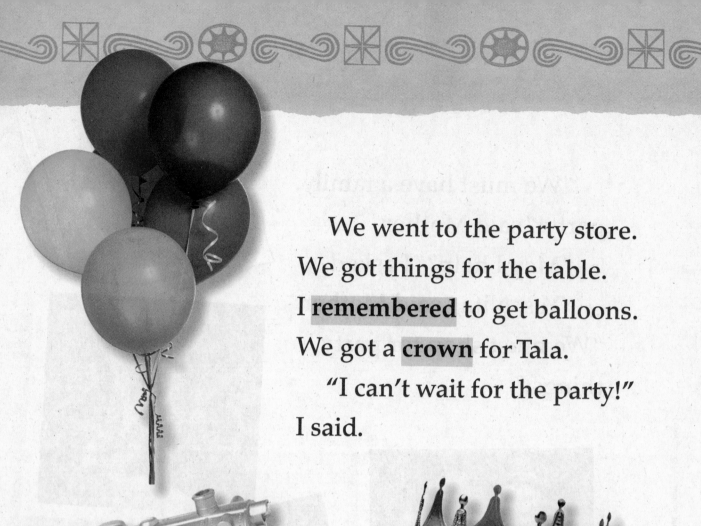

We went to the party store.
We got things for the table.
I **remembered** to get balloons.
We got a **crown** for Tala.

"I can't wait for the party!"
I said.

UNDERSTANDING CHARACTERS

How does Nita feel?

_____

_____

_____

"We have more shopping
to do," said Mother.
We went to the toy store.
I saw a stuffed bear. We got it
for my **cousin** Tala.

Stop | **Think** | **Write**

VOCABULARY

The bear is for Nita's _____ Tala.

We went to the market next. We got fruit. We got vegetables. We got other good things to eat.

We put the food in our cart. Soon we had all we needed.

Stop | **Think** | **Write**

CAUSE AND EFFECT

Why do Mother and Nita go to the market?

_____

_____

_____

Then we went home. Mother cooked. I helped. "It smells so good!" I said.

We put out the party things. "Now we are ready!" said Mother.

Stop | **Think** | **Write**

Mother and Nita cook. Then they are

_____ for the party.

It was party time! Everyone in our family came. We ate. We laughed. My aunt played music. Tala wore her crown.

"This is a special party!" said Uncle Takada. "Thank you!"

Stop | Think | Write

COMPARE AND CONTRAST

How are the people at the party alike?

_____

_____

_____

Look Back and Respond

1 How do you know that Nita is excited to meet Tala?

Hint

For clues, see pages 16 and 17.

_____

_____

_____

2 How are the party store and the market different?

Hint

For clues, see pages 16 and 18.

_____

_____

_____

3 Who played music at the party?

Hint

For a clue, see page 20.

_____

busy

chipmunks

turned

woods

Hiking on a Fall Day

Check the answer.

1 Let's go hiking! Where can we go? We can walk in the _____. We will have trees all around us.

☐ **woods** ☐ **chipmunks** ☐ **collars**

2 It is a beautiful fall day. The leaves are not green anymore. They have _____ gold.

☐ **drooled** ☐ **stood** ☐ **turned**

3 Let's look for animals. We see little
_____. They are brown. They have
stripes. They run fast.

☐ **stories**   ☐ **chipmunks**   ☐ **places**

4 What things can you see in the
<u>woods</u>?

_____

_____

_____

5 Tell about a time when you were
<u>busy</u>.

_____

_____

_____

Too Little for Camping

by Claire Daniel

Uncle Juan is taking me camping! I like camping.

My sister Malia wants to go, too. I don't want her to come. I think Malia is too little for camping.

Stop | Think | Write

UNDERSTANDING CHARACTERS

Malia wants to go _____.

24

"Camping is hard," I say. "You have to go fishing. We will sleep in the **woods**."

Malia says, "I want to fish. I like the woods."

Malia comes with us.

Stop | Think | Write

VOCABULARY

Malia will camp in the

_____.

25

We hike in the woods. Malia says, "I'm tired."

We set up the tent. "This is hard!" says Malia.

"You are too little for camping," I say.

Stop **Think** **Write**

SEQUENCE OF EVENTS

After the hike, they set up the

_____.

"It's time to fish now," says Uncle Juan. We go to the lake. Uncle Juan puts a worm on a hook.

"Yuck!" Malia says.

"You are too little to fish," I say.

STORY STRUCTURE

Malia and her brother fish at the

_____.

Soon a fish tugs on Malia's line. Malia catches a very big fish. I help. "Maybe you are not too little to fish," I say. "You caught our dinner!"

AUTHOR'S PURPOSE

How can you tell Malia's brother is starting to be happy that Malia is there?

_____

_____

_____

We go back to the tent. We see two **chipmunks**. They run around the tent. We laugh and laugh.

Uncle Juan cooks the fish. We eat it after it has **turned** brown. It tastes great!

Stop Think Write

AUTHOR'S PURPOSE

How do you think the author wants us to feel when we read about the <u>chipmunks</u>? Explain.

_____

_____

_____

29

The next day we go home. We hike to the car. "I had fun," Malia says. "We were **busy**! I am glad that I came."

"I am glad, too," I say. "You are a great camper, Malia."

Stop | Think | Write

VOCABULARY

Malia and her brother are

_____ during the trip.

Look Back and Respond

1 Why doesn't the boy want Malia to go camping?

Hint
For clues, see page 24.

_____

_____

_____

2 What happens to Malia's fish?

Hint
For clues, see pages 28 and 29.

_____

_____

_____

3 Did the author write this story to entertain readers or to give information? How can you tell?

Hint
How do you feel when you read the story?

_____

_____

_____

Different Kinds of Places

① A **dangerous** place isn't right for you. A street is dangerous. It isn't safe. You might get hurt.

Name a <u>dangerous</u> place.

_____

_____

② Some places might **scare** you. No one likes to be afraid. Scary places are not right for you!

Name two places that might <u>scare</u> a cat.

_____

_____

3 Noisy places aren't much fun. People might be **screaming**. It's hard to like a noisy place.

Name a noisy place where people might be <u>screaming</u>.

_____

_____

4 Is a quiet place right for you? Do you like to hear the birds sing? Do you like to hear the **breeze** blow?

Name a place where you might hear the <u>breeze</u>.

_____

_____

Diva the Dancer

by Duncan Searl

Diva was a dog. She was also a dancer. Diva needed a job.

"Maybe I can work at the circus," Diva said.

Diva went to the circus. She asked for a job dancing.

Stop **Think** **Write**

CAUSE AND EFFECT

Diva went to the circus to get a

_____ .

34

The circus people had only one kind of job. "Work up here with us," they said.

Diva shook her head. "Those jobs look **dangerous**! I just want to dance."

Stop	Think	Write

The circus job looked _____ to Diva.

Diva went to Officer Lee for a job. "You can help me catch bad guys," said Officer Lee.

"No, thanks," said Diva. "That might **scare** me. Besides, I want to dance."

VOCABULARY

What kind of people <u>scare</u> Diva?

_____

_____

_____

Mr. Ray wanted a nice quiet pet. Diva got the job. Diva was happy. She began to dance.

"No dancing!" Mr. Ray said. "I want peace and quiet!" So Diva moved on.

Stop Think Write

CAUSE AND EFFECT

Diva left Mr. Ray because she could not

_____ there.

Mrs. Bibb wanted a dog for her boys. "I'm great with children," Diva told her.

The Bibb boys weren't great for Diva. They were always **screaming**. There was too much noise for Diva to dance.

Stop | Think | Write

VOCABULARY

The Bibb boys made noise by

_____.

Diva left the Bibbs. Outside, she heard music in the **breeze**.

Diva followed the music. She came to a house. It was near a park.

Stop Think Write

STORY STRUCTURE

The music came from a _____.

The house was a dance school.

"I need a helper," the teacher told Diva.
"Can you dance?"

Diva began to dance. And she's been
dancing ever since.

STORY STRUCTURE

Diva got a job at a _____

Look Back and Respond

1 **Why did Diva go to the circus?**

Hint
For a clue, see page 34.

_____

_____

_____

2 **Why did Diva leave the Bibbs?**

Hint
For a clue, see page 38.

_____

_____

_____

3 **Did Diva get the right job in the end? How do you know?**

Hint
For a clue, see page 40.

_____

_____

_____

noticed

quiet

share

wonderful

The Sandbox

1 I was playing in the park. I **noticed** a new boy.

Have you ever <u>noticed</u> a new student at school? Explain.

_____

_____

_____

2 I did not want to play with him. He was too **quiet**.

Name a place where people need to be <u>quiet</u>.

_____

_____

_____

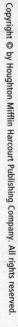

3 The new boy came over to me.
Mom gave me a look. I had to **share**
my toys.

What was the last thing that you
had to <u>share</u>?

_____

_____

_____

4 The boy's name was Mark. He built
a cool castle. We played together.
We had a **wonderful** time.

Name something that smells
<u>wonderful</u> to you.

_____

_____

_____

43

The New Playground

by Jason Powe

"I have some **wonderful** news," says
Mrs. Ruiz. "You will help plan the new
playground!"

"A new playground?" asks Paul.

"That will be fun!" says Rosa.

Stop | Think | Write

STORY STRUCTURE

What will the children plan?

_____

_____

_____

44

Mrs. Ruiz takes the children to her office. Their teacher, Mr. Jones, is there, too. The room is **quiet**.

"How do we begin?" asks Paul.

Stop **Think** **Write**

VOCABULARY

The room is not loud. It is

_____ .

"Think about what you like to do outside," says Mrs. Ruiz. "Then talk about your ideas."

"We all have to agree," says Mr. Jones.

Stop | Think | Write

STORY STRUCTURE

What does Mrs. Ruiz want the children to think about?

_____

_____

_____

Each child thinks. Rosa loves to swing. Lucy thinks of shooting hoops. Paul dreams of playing in the sand.

They write down their ideas. Then it is time to **share**.

Stop **Think** **Write**

MAIN IDEAS AND DETAILS

The children will share their

_____ with each other.

"I **noticed** that we don't have swings,"
says Rosa. "Let's get some!"

"I want a basketball court," says Lucy.

"A sandbox, too!" says Paul.

| Stop | Think | Write |

Rosa _____ that they don't
have swings.

48

Mrs. Ruiz listens. "I like those ideas," she says.

It takes time to build the playground. The children dream about what it will look like.

Stop **Think** **Write**

STORY STRUCTURE

Why does Mrs. Ruiz listen to the children?

_____

_____

_____

49

At last, the playground is ready. It has a sandbox. It has swings. It even has a hoop!

The whole school loves the new playground. The children did a good job.

Stop | **Think** | **Write**

Where are the children at the end of the story?

_____

_____

_____

Look Back and Respond

1 What is Mrs. Ruiz's wonderful news?

_____

_____

_____

Hint

For a clue, see page 44.

2 Where do the children meet to plan the playground?

_____

_____

_____

Hint

For a clue, see page 45.

3 Imagine you are planning a playground. What kinds of things would you like?

_____

_____

_____

Hint

Think about what you like to do outside.

branches

deepest

pond

winding

Nature

Check the answer.

1 The river is _____.
It curves left. It curves right.

☐ **straight** ☐ **winding** ☐ **weighed**

2 The _____ part of the ocean is almost seven miles below the surface.

☐ **deepest** ☐ **busy** ☐ **winding**

3 Frogs and turtles live in water. They could live in a _____.

☐ **piano** ☐ **porch** ☐ **pond**

4 What happens to a tree's <u>branches</u> on a windy day?

_____

_____

_____

5 What is the <u>deepest</u> water you have been in?

_____

_____

Who Made These?

by John Berry

Snow fell. Now the tree **branches** are white. Molly and her brother take a walk.

"How will we know where to go?" asks Jeff. "Snow has covered the path."

"Don't worry," says Molly. "I can find the way. I know these woods."

| Stop | Think | Write |

TEXT AND GRAPHIC FEATURES

Who made the tracks in the snow on this page?

_____

_____

_____

They walk across their yard. Jeff stops.
He points to some tracks.

"Who made these?" he asks.

"Here is a hint. It is an animal that
hops," Molly says. "It has a round tail."

Stop | **Think** | **Write**

TEXT AND GRAPHIC FEATURES

Jeff points to some tracks. The tracks are in the

_____.

"A rabbit?" Jeff asks.

"Right," Molly says. "It was a cottontail rabbit."

They walk into the woods. They go around trees. They go over hills. They go left and right. The path is **winding**.

rabbit

Stop | Think | Write

VOCABULARY

The path isn't straight. It's _____.

They come to a **pond**. Jeff finds more tracks.

"Who made these?" he asks.

"An animal with a black mask," Molly says. "It has a striped tail."

Stop **Think** **Write**

TEXT AND GRAPHIC FEATURES

How does the reader know when someone is speaking?

_____

_____

_____

"A raccoon?" Jeff asks.

"Right again!" Molly says.

"I saw a raccoon last fall," Jeff says. "It was up in our apple tree. I guess it liked apples."

Molly and Jeff move on.

raccoon

Stop **Think** **Write**

CAUSE AND EFFECT

Jeff saw a raccoon in a tree. He thought it liked

_____.

They cross a field. Molly points to more tracks.

"These are the **deepest** tracks," Jeff says. "They go far down into the snow. Who made them?"

"A big animal," Molly says. "It has antlers."

| Stop | Think | Write | VOCABULARY |

Why do you think these tracks are the deepest?

_____

_____

59

"A deer?" Jeff asks.

"Right again," Molly says. "These are the tracks of a big deer."

"How do you know so much?" Jeff asks.

"I'm older," Molly says. "Soon you'll be a great tracker, too."

deer

Stop   Think   Write

CONCLUSIONS

Do you think Molly is a good older sister? Tell why or why not.

Look Back and Respond

1 How many toes does a raccoon have on each foot?

Hint
For clues, see pages 57 and 58.

_____

_____

_____

2 How are rabbit tracks and deer tracks different?

Hint
For clues, see pages 56 and 60.

_____

_____

_____

3 What does Jeff learn on the walk?

Hint
For clues, see pages 55 through 60.

_____

_____

_____

✓ TARGET VOCABULARY

blooming

plain

scent

shovels

In the Garden

1 Roses are **blooming** in the garden. New flowers grow each year.

What season is it when flowers and trees are <u>blooming</u>?

_____

_____

_____

2 The roses have a sweet **scent**. Many people like to smell them.

Name something outside that has a sweet <u>scent</u>.

_____

_____

_____

3 The apple tree looks **plain** in winter. It does not have leaves or flowers. The tree blooms in spring. Then it looks dressed up!

Name two things that can look plain.

_____

_____

_____

4 In the garden, people use **shovels**. They are good for breaking up the dirt.

What are some jobs that <u>shovels</u> could help you do?

_____

_____

_____

Rosa's Garden

by Carol Alexander

I am Sofia. This is Miss Rosa.
She has a garden. It is big!
Miss Rosa grows flowers.
She grows carrots and peas.
I don't eat peas. Not one pea.
No way!

Stop **Think** **Write**

CONCLUSIONS

Who do you think planted the garden? Why?

_____

_____

_____

64

This summer, Miss Rosa fell. She hurt her knee. Now she can't walk. She just sits in a chair. She watches the birds.

Two **shovels** lie in the grass. Miss Rosa looks sad. What would help her feel better?

Stop **Think** **Write**

What could help Miss Rosa feel better?

_____

_____

_____

I go home to think. "Mom, I need paper. I want to draw a picture."

Mom smiles. "Here is some **plain** white paper." She gives me a few pieces. "I can't wait to see what you draw."

Stop **Think** **Write**

Sofia's paper has no lines. It is

_____.

I find my crayons. What will I draw?
I close my eyes. The **scent** of flowers
blows in through the window. Now I
know just what to draw.

Stop | Think | Write

CONCLUSIONS

What do you think Sofia will draw?

_____

_____

_____

I draw and draw. Here are the sweet peas. They are **blooming** in May. There are the tomatoes. They are red and round.

I keep drawing. Mom says, "Your hand will fall off, Sofia!"

Stop **Think** **Write**

VOCABULARY

The flowers are _____ in Sofia's picture.

At last, I am done. I find Miss Rosa.
I hand her my picture.

"This is for you," I say.

She looks at it. She smiles and
hugs me.

"Do you really like it?" I ask.

Stop **Think** **Write**

CONCLUSIONS

Does Miss Rosa like the drawing? Explain.

_____

_____

_____

"Oh, yes!" Miss Rosa says. "This is the best garden. It makes me happy. Thank you, Sofia."

"Spring will come again. We can work in the garden together," I say. "We will plant lots of peas!"

Stop | **Think** | **Write**

The picture makes Miss Rosa feel

_____ .

70

Look Back and Respond

1 Why does Miss Rosa feel sad?

_____

_____

Hint
For a clue, see page 65.

2 Why does Sofia draw a picture?

_____

_____

_____

Hint
For a clue, see page 65.

3 Why does Miss Rosa like the picture?

_____

_____

_____

Hint
For a clue, see page 70.

beware

damage

pounding

prevent

When a Storm Comes

1 Storms can come fast.

_____ of strong winds! Watch out for dark clouds. They bring rain.

2 Storms can _____ buildings. Windows can break. A roof can blow off!

3 _____ rain hits the ground hard. Flowers are knocked over. Tree branches break.

4 We can take steps to _____ a storm from hurting us. We can stay inside. We can stay away from windows and doors.

Write the vocabulary word that best completes the synonym web.

5

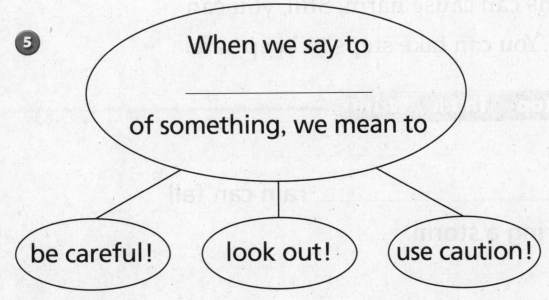

When we say to _____ of something, we mean to

be careful!

look out!

use caution!

Keeping Safe in a Storm

by Carol Alexander

Big storms can be scary. Strong winds are loud. They shake things. **Pounding** rain falls.

Storms can cause harm. Still, you can prepare. You can take steps to keep safe.

Stop   Think   Write

A _____ rain can fall during a storm.

74

Planning

You should plan ahead. Find safe places at home. They should be away from windows and doors.

You may need supplies. You can put water in bottles. You can freeze food. Make sure you have candles, too.

Stop **Think** **Write**

MAIN IDEAS AND DETAILS

Storing _____ in bottles can be part of a plan for **staying safe**.

Before a Storm

You can learn about a storm that is coming. Just listen to the TV or radio. Experts watch the path of storms. News reporters warn people about bad storms.

Some storms are very strong. It may not be safe to stay at home. You may have to go to a safer place.

Stop   Think   Write

CAUSE AND EFFECT

If a storm is very _____,
you may not be able to stay at home.

You can **prevent** problems at home. Bring toys and pets inside. Put garbage cans where wind can't tip them over.

Wind can **damage** windows. Some people tape windows. Tape makes them stronger.

Stop Think Write

VOCABULARY

Storms can _____ windows.
Taping windows helps to protect them.

During a Storm

The storm hits! You should not go outside. Find a safe place inside.

You can play games. Don't play games that use electricity. Things that use electricity can be dangerous in storms. **Beware** of computers. Do not talk on the phone.

| Stop | Think | Write |

Games that don't use _____
are safe to play during a storm.

After a Storm

Listen to the news. Reporters will tell you when it is safe to go outside.

You must still be careful. Stay away from damaged trees. Ask a grownup where you can play.

Isn't it good to be outside again?

Stop | Think | Write

MAIN IDEAS AND DETAILS

Listen to the _____ to find out when it is safe to go outside after a storm.

79

Kinds of Storms

A **blizzard** is a bad winter storm. It has big winds. It has lots of snow.

A **tornado** is a tube of wind. It can pick up a house!

A **hurricane** is a storm from the sea. It has big winds and waves. It can cause bad floods.

Stop Think Write

COMPARE AND CONTRAST

Write one way all these storms are alike.

_____

_____

_____

Look Back and Respond

1 What are two things you can do to plan ahead for storms?

Hint

For clues, look on page 75.

_____

_____

_____

2 How can you protect your home?

Hint

For clues, look on page 77.

_____

_____

_____

3 How can you tell when it is safe to go outside after a storm?

Hint

For a clue, look on page 79.

_____

_____

_____

curled

direction

height

toward

A Forest

1 A forest is full of trees. The **height** of each tree is different. Some trees are taller than others.

Name something with a <u>height</u> that's greater than your school's.

_____

_____

_____

2 There are other plants in a forest. Vines are **curled** around the trees.

Name an animal that you've seen <u>curled</u> up.

_____

_____

82

3 There are animals in the forest. It is hard to see them. People scare them. Then the animals run in a different **direction**.

Name two things that would make you run in a different direction.

_____

_____

4 You may see an animal in the forest. Be quiet. Be still. Don't move **toward** it.

Why isn't it a good idea to move toward a wild animal?

_____

_____

Tortoise Gets a Home
by Jake Harris

Forest loved the animals. She gave each one a home.

Lizard got a rock home. Crab got a hole in the sand. Forest forgot all about Tortoise.

Stop | Think | Write

UNDERSTANDING CHARACTERS

What does Forest do?

_____

_____

_____

84

Snake **curled** up under leaves. Owl sat in a hole in a tree.

The animals thanked Forest. They were all happy. All but Tortoise! Tortoise was sad.

Stop | **Think** | **Write**

VOCABULARY

Snake likes to be _____ up in his home.

One night, a storm came. Tortoise had no home. He needed to find one. He needed to stay warm and dry.

Tortoise saw a hole in some rocks. Lizard looked out. "Sorry, my house is too small for you," she said.

CAUSE AND EFFECT

Why can't Lizard share her house with Tortoise?

_____

_____

_____

Tortoise walked **toward** a hole in the sand. Crab popped his head out.

Tortoise tried to crawl under some leaves. "I'm under here!" said Snake.

Stop | **Think** | **Write**

VOCABULARY

Tortoise walks _____

Crab's home.

Tortoise went in the **direction** of a tall tree. Owl hooted at him to go away. The tree was the right **height** for Owl. It was too tall for Tortoise.

Tortoise did not want to be in the rain. Then he found a broken coconut shell.

Stop | Think | Write

Tortoise does not want _____.

Tortoise crawled under the shell. He pulled in his legs. He pulled in his neck. It was just big enough to cover him. Tortoise was warm and dry.

In the morning, the rain had gone. Tortoise came out from his shell. Forest saw him.

Stop Think Write

What does Tortoise do during the storm?

_____

_____

_____

"Tortoise!" said Forest. "I am sorry. I forgot to give you a home. I see you found one. This shell will stay on your back. Your home will always be with you."

Today, all tortoises have shells.

Stop | **Think** | **Write**

Forest is _____ she forgot about Tortoise.

Look Back and Respond

1 How does Tortoise feel at the beginning of the story? Why?

Hint

For clues, see pages 84 and 85.

_____

_____

_____

2 Why does Tortoise need a home?

Hint

See page 86.

_____

_____

_____

3 How do you think Tortoise feels at the end of the story? Why?

Hint

For clues, see pages 89 and 90.

_____

_____

_____

✓ TARGET VOCABULARY

choices
disgusting
millions
weaker

Trash in Our Oceans

Check the answer.

1 _____ of plastic bags go into the ocean. They hurt animals that live there.
- ☐ **Muscles**
- ☐ **Weaker**
- ☐ **Millions**

2 Trash in the ocean is _____. It traps fish. It makes them sick.
- ☐ screaming
- ☐ disgusting
- ☐ weaker

3 A fish can get stuck in a bag. The fish can get hurt. It cannot find food. The fish gets _____.

☐ **millions** ☐ **direction** ☐ **weaker**

4 What are some <u>choices</u> that you have today?

_____

_____

_____

5 Name something that you can count in the <u>millions</u>.

_____

At the Beach

by John Berry

Max collects shells. He knows all about them. He says that **millions** of animals have shells.

He takes me to the beach. Max is excited. He wants to find a conch shell.

Stop Think Write

VOCABULARY

Max says that there are _____ of animals with shells.

We get to the beach. Max gets upset.
He finds trash in the sand.

"This is **disgusting**!" he says. "People
should not litter."

I agree.

Stop | **Think** | **Write**

Trash on a beach isn't nice. Max thinks it is

_____.

We look for shells. First we find rocks. Then we find sticks. At last we find shells.

"Look at this one," I say.

"I have one like that," Max says. "See?"

MAIN IDEAS AND DETAILS

The boys find _____ at the beach.

He pulls a shell from his bag. It is the same. I toss my shell into the sea.

"Hey! A crab!" I say.

"It has two claws," Max says. "The big one is strong. The small one is **weaker**."

Stop **Think** **Write**

FACT AND OPINION

One fact about the crab is that it has

_____.

"There's another crab," I say. "It looks funny."

"That's a hermit crab," says Max. "They find shells to live in. This crab doesn't have a shell."

"You can give him a shell," I say.

Stop Think Write

The boy says that the crab looks funny. Is that a fact or an opinion?

_____

_____

"Hermit crabs live in snail shells," says Max. "I have only one snail shell."

"Well, you have two **choices**," I say. "You can give the crab a home or keep the shell."

Stop **Think** **Write**

FACT AND OPINION

Max says that hermit crabs live in snail shells. Is that a fact or an opinion?

_____

_____

I walk away. I look back. Max puts the shell on the sand. The crab goes in. Max looks happy.

I'm happy, too.

Stop **Think** **Write**

STORY STRUCTURE

What choice does Max make?

_____

_____

_____

Look Back and Respond

1 Look at page 95. Write one sentence that is an opinion.

Hint

Remember that an opinion shows what someone thinks or feels.

_____

_____

_____

2 Write one fact that Max tells about shells.

Hint

For clues, see pages 94, 98, and 99.

_____

_____

_____

3 If you were Max, which choice would you have made?

Hint

Think about Max's choices. Think about what Max wants.

_____

_____

_____

Lesson 11

✓ TARGET VOCABULARY

believe

furious

impossible

problem

Getting Along

1 Mia wants to draw a cat. Leo shows her how. He breaks her chalk. Now Mia is very mad.

She is _____

with Leo.

2 Leo says, "I'm very sorry. I can't fix your chalk. That's

_____."

102

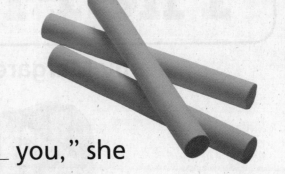

3 Mia feels better. "I

_____ you," she

says. "I know you are sorry."

4 "I can fix the

_____," Leo tells

Mia. He gives her his chalk.

**Write the vocabulary word that best
completes the synonym web.**

5

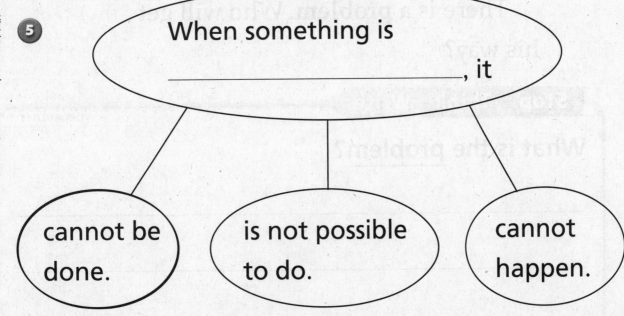

When something is _____, it

cannot be done.

is not possible to do.

cannot happen.

The Play Date

by Margaret Maugenest

Eric and Dylan are brothers. Raul comes to play with them.

"Let's make a spaceship," says Dylan.

"Let's play baseball," says Eric.

There is a **problem**. Who will get his way?

Stop Think Write

VOCABULARY

What is the problem?

_____

_____

_____

"I have an idea," says Raul. Let's build
a spaceship first. Then we can play ball."

Eric gets **furious**. "No," he says.

"Making a spaceship is a baby game."

Eric goes to his room. He slams the door.

Stop **Think** **Write**

CONCLUSIONS

How can you tell that Eric is mad?

_____

_____

_____

105

Raul frowns. "Let's make the spaceship. Eric will calm down. He can come later," Raul says.

Dylan and Raul go to Dylan's room. Eric hears them laugh. He puts his ear to the wall.

CONCLUSIONS

Two friends, _____ and

_____ , are having a good

time.

Eric hears talking.

"This is fun," says Raul.

"I wish Eric were here," says Dylan.

Eric wants to play. It is **impossible** for him to stay mad. He goes to Dylan's room. He peeks inside.

Stop Think Write

VOCABULARY

It is _____ for Eric to stay angry.

Eric sees the spaceship. Dylan and
Raul are in it.

"Blast off!" says Dylan.

"Is there room for me?" says Eric.

CONCLUSIONS

What does Eric want to do?

_____

_____

_____

Dylan and Raul smile.

"Yes! Get in," says Raul. "We're off to the Moon."

Eric sits in the tent. "I'm sorry I got mad," he says.

Stop **Think** **Write**

CONCLUSIONS

Dylan and Raul feel _____ when Eric comes.

"We didn't **believe** you would stay mad," says Raul.

"We'll play ball soon. We just have to get back from the Moon!" says Dylan.

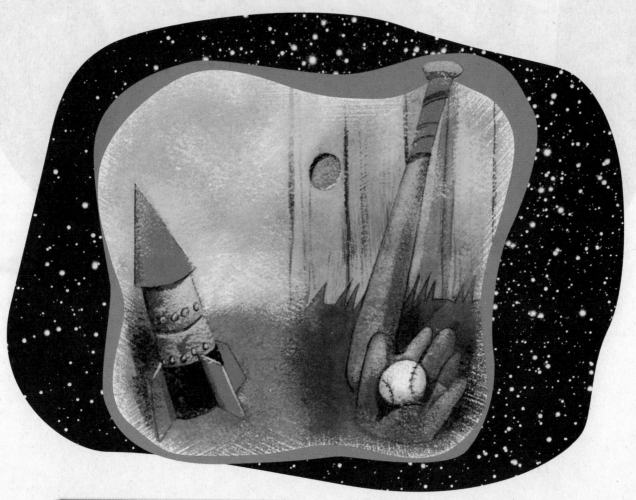

Stop **Think** **Write**

STORY STRUCTURE

They will all play _____ later.

110

Look Back and Respond

1 **Why is Eric mad?**

Hint

For clues, see pages 104 and 105.

_____

_____

_____

2 **Eric puts his ear to the wall. Why?**

Hint

For clues, see pages 106 and 107.

_____

_____

3 **Is Raul good at getting along? How do you know?**

Hint

See pages 105, 106, 109, and 110.

_____

_____

_____

alone

hours

smooth

whenever

Singers

Do you like to sing? Some people sing for their job. Some are famous!

Singers can sing with others. They can also sing **alone**.

Singers have to practice. They want to get better. They can spend **hours** singing. They sing **whenever** they can.

A good singer has a **smooth** voice. It is even. It is nice to hear.

1 A singer can sing

_____ or with other
people.

2 Singers have to work hard. They

practice for _____.

3 A good singer has a

_____, even voice.

4 Tell what you do <u>whenever</u> you
hear music.

_____

_____

_____

Val's Voice

by Claire Daniel

Val loved to sing. She sang **alone**.
She sang to her family. She sang to her
friends. She sang for **hours**.

There was one problem. Her voice
was very loud.

Stop Think Write

Val loves to sing. She sings

for _____.

Val went to a party. It was time to sing. Val sang. Her friends sang, too. One voice was loudest. It was Val's! Val's friends were not happy. Val's voice was too loud.

Stop | Think | Write

STORY STRUCTURE

At the party, Val sings in a

_____ **voice.**

Val's mom went to see Val's teacher. "**Whenever** Val sings, her voice is too loud. What can we do?"

Mr. Hendricks said, "She can join the chorus. She can learn to sing softly."

Stop **Think** **Write**

STORY STRUCTURE

Mr. Hendricks thinks Val should sing in the _____.

Val joined the chorus. Her friends sang in the chorus, too.

Val raised her hand. She said, "I love to sing. I want to be a famous singer!"

"That's good!" Ms. Seal said.

Stop Think Write

STORY STRUCTURE

Val tells Ms. Seal that she wants to be a famous

_____.

"We will have a concert soon,"
Ms. Seal said. "We must work hard."

The chorus sang. Val's friends were
not happy. Ms. Seal was not happy.
The only voice they
could hear was Val's!

Stop | Think | Write

At chorus, the children could only hear

_____ **voice.**

Ms. Seal said, "Val, do you want to be a good singer?" Val nodded.

"Good singers make a **smooth** sound," said Ms. Seal. "They use a loud voice. They use a soft voice, too." Ms. Seal showed her how.

Stop **Think** **Write**

VOCABULARY

Ms. Seal shows Val how to make a

_____ **sound.**

119

The day of the concert came. The chorus sang their songs. Val's voice was soft. Then Val sang a song alone. Val's voice was smooth. It was soft and loud. Val had learned how to sing!

Stop   Think   Write

INFER AND PREDICT

Val sings well in the _____.

Look Back and Respond

1 **What is the problem in the story?**

Hint

For a clue, see page 114.

_____

_____

_____

2 **How does Val change her singing to make it better?**

Hint

For clues, see pages 119 and 120.

_____

_____

_____

3 **How does the story end?**

Hint

For a clue, see page 120.

_____

_____

_____

community

culture

special

wear

Ball Games

1 Kids like to play with balls. You can bounce a ball. You can throw a ball. All the kids in a **community** can play.

What kinds of ball games do kids in your <u>community</u> play?

_____

_____

_____

2 Ball games are part of a culture. Music and food are part of a **culture**, too.

Name a food that is part of your <u>culture</u>.

_____

122

3 Players **wear** uniforms in many ball games.

What is your favorite thing to <u>wear</u>?

_____

_____

_____

4 Dodge ball is a game. It has **special** rules. You can hit someone with the ball. Then the person is out.

What are the <u>special</u> rules of your favorite game?

_____

_____

_____

Game Time!

by John Berry

What games do you play? Do you play with a ball? Do you play board games?

Kids play all over the world. Every **culture** has its own games. There are many ways to have fun!

Stop Think Write

VOCABULARY

Games are part of a country's

_____ .

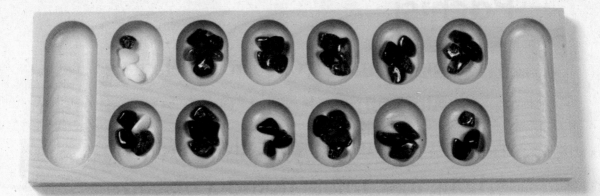

Mancala

Mancala is a counting game. It was first played in Africa. You can play with seeds. You can play with stones.

Players pick up the stones. They drop them into the bins. It seems easy, but it is hard to play well!

Stop | **Think** | **Write**

AUTHOR'S PURPOSE

The author wants us to know that mancala is

_____ **to play well.**

Pachisi

Pachisi comes from India. Players move pieces on a board. Each player wants to get to the middle first.

Long ago, rulers in India played pachisi. Today, people play in other countries, too.

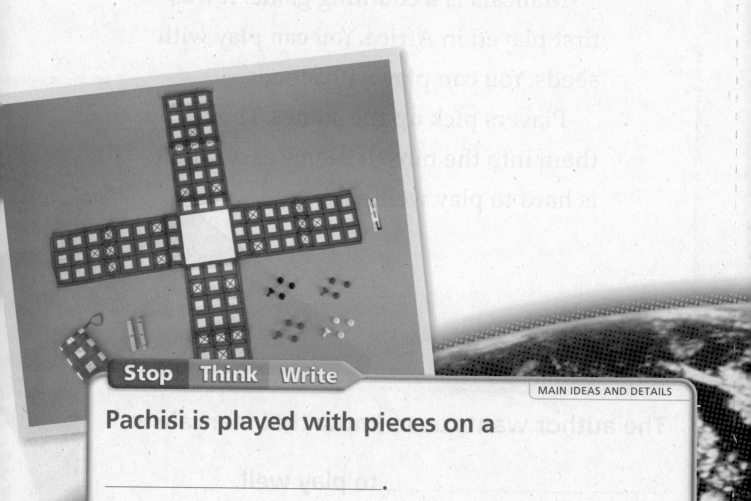

MAIN IDEAS AND DETAILS

Pachisi is played with pieces on a

_____.

Games with String

The Inuit are native people. They are from North America. People in the Inuit **community** learn to make string shapes. It is their tradition.

Children all over play games with string. Cat's Cradle is one string game.

Stop	Think	Write	AUTHOR'S PURPOSE

The author wants to inform readers about Inuit

_____ shapes.

Soccer

People all over the world play soccer. More people play soccer than any other game!

Players run. They kick the ball. They cannot touch it with their hands. Players often **wear** uniforms.

Stop **Think** **Write**

VOCABULARY

Soccer players can _____

uniforms.

128

A Battle Game

A game was invented in China. It is hundreds of years old. It is played with stones on a board. The game is called Go.

The game is a battle. Players trap each other's stones. They must plan well. It takes skill to win!

Stop	Think	Write

CONCLUSIONS

Players trap each other's stones. It is like a

_____.

Marbles

Long ago, children in Egypt played a game with marbles. Kids still play marbles today. Kids collect marbles, too.

Marbles come in many colors. Some **special** marbles are called cat's eyes. They sparkle like the eyes of a cat.

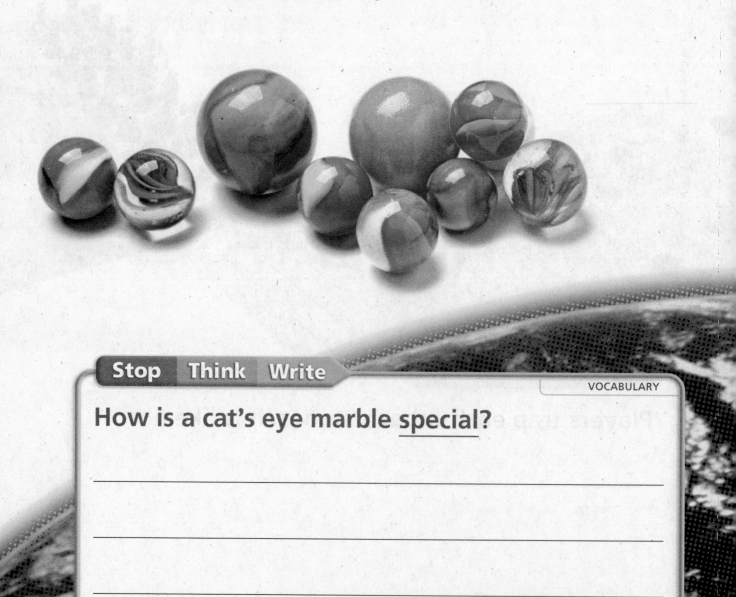

Stop   Think   Write

How is a cat's eye marble **special**?

_____

_____

_____

Look Back and Respond

1 What is the most popular game in the world?

Hint
For a hint, see page 128.

_____

2 How are Go and pachisi alike?

Hint
For hints, see pages 126 and 129.

_____

_____

_____

3 Did the author write this text to entertain readers or to give information?

Hint
Did you learn something new?

_____

_____

_____

✔ TARGET VOCABULARY

curious

darkness

knowledge

motion

The Senses

1 The five senses are sight, hearing, smell, taste, and touch. They give us **knowledge** of the world.

What knowledge can you get from hearing something?

_____

_____

_____

2 When we are **curious** about something, we use our senses. We look, listen, feel, or smell to learn more.

What are you curious about?

_____

_____

_____

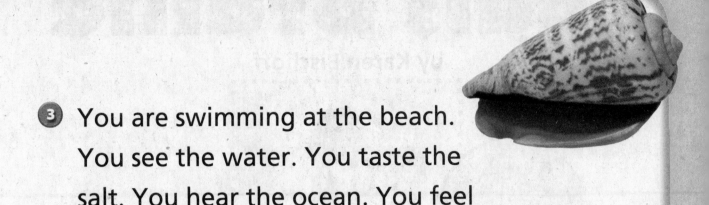

3 You are swimming at the beach. You see the water. You taste the salt. You hear the ocean. You feel the **motion** of the waves.

What other <u>motion</u> might you see at the beach?

_____

_____

_____

4 You can hear things at night. You can feel and smell at night. You might not see well in the **darkness**.

Write a word that means the opposite of <u>darkness</u>.

_____

Louis Braille

by Karen Bischoff

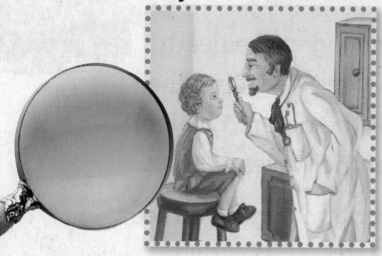

Louis Braille was born two hundred years ago. He became blind at the age of three. He lived in a world of **darkness** from then on.

Louis was smart. He tried to do well at school. However, he could not read. He could not write. Louis had to leave school. Still, he wanted to learn.

Stop. Think Write

CAUSE AND EFFECT

School was hard for Louis because he was

_____.

A Special School

Louis got a lucky break. He joined a special school. It was for children who could not see. He learned a lot there.

Louis was **curious**. He wanted to learn more. He wanted the **knowledge** he could get from books.

Stop | Think | Write

VOCABULARY

Louis wanted to read books. This shows that he

was _____.

135

Louis Gets an Idea

Louis was blind, but he could feel with his fingers. He had an idea to make writing that people could feel. He thought of letters made of dots. They would be little bumps on the paper.

Stop Think Write

Why did Louis want to make special letters?

_____

_____

_____

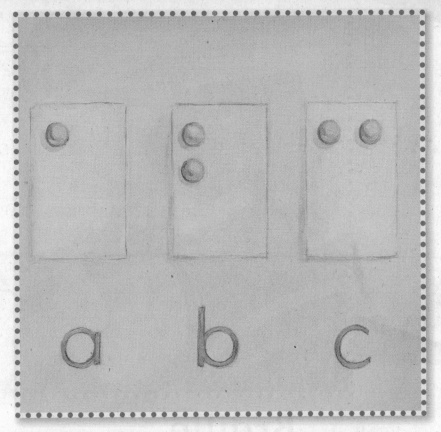

Louis took paper. He made little bumps on it. Each set of bumps was a letter. When he joined the letters, he made words. Louis was writing!

Louis made a **motion** over the bumps with his fingers. He could feel the bumps. He was reading with his hands!

Stop Think Write

VOCABULARY

Tell about the hand <u>motion</u> Louis made.

_____

_____

_____

Braille

Louis was only 15 years old. He made an alphabet for blind people. That alphabet is now called braille.

His idea let him write. It let other blind people read what he wrote. He started to make books written in braille.

Stop **Think** **Write**

MAIN IDEAS AND DETAILS

Who needed Louis' alphabet?

Helping Others

Louis stayed at the school. He became a teacher. He showed children how to read in braille. He showed them how to write in braille.

The children loved Louis. He opened the door to a new world for them.

Stop **Think** **Write**

INFER AND PREDICT

What was the new world that Louis introduced?

_____

_____

_____

Braille Today

Today, you can find braille books in stores and in libraries. People all over the world read braille.

Many people cannot see. Thanks to Louis Braille, they can read and write.

Stop **Think** **Write**

Why are reading and writing important?

_____

_____

_____

Look Back and Respond

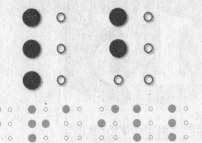

L O U I S   B R A I L L E

1 **What is this story mostly about?**

_____

_____

_____

Hint

You must read every page to answer this.

2 **What is braille?**

_____

_____

_____

Hint

For clues, see pages 138 and 139.

3 **Why is braille helpful?**

_____

_____

_____

Hint

Look on pages 138, 139, and 140.

buddy

safety

speech

station

Safety at the Beach

1 Lifeguards work at the beach. They watch the swimmers from a **station**.

Name another kind of <u>station</u>.

_____

2 A lifeguard gave a **speech**. She told us how to be safe in the ocean.

Think about a <u>speech</u> you would like to give. What would you talk about?

_____

_____

_____

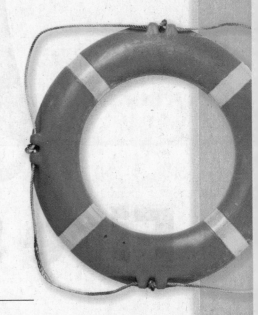

3 Don't take chances at the beach. Stay out of danger. Follow the **safety** rules.

Name a good <u>safety</u> rule for the beach.

_____

_____

_____

4 You should never swim alone. Always swim with a **buddy**.

What is something you like to do with a <u>buddy</u>?

_____

_____

_____

Fire Safety Day

by John Berry

Randy walked to school. He was glad.
His class had gym today. He loved gym.
They would play games. They would
kick balls. Best of all, they would tumble.
Randy was ready to practice somersaults
and cartwheels.

Stop | **Think** | **Write**

UNDERSTANDING CHARACTERS

Randy is excited to go to school because he

wants to _____.

When he got to the gym, the gray mats were not out. They were stacked against the wall.

Mrs. Nelson was standing with two people from the fire **station**.

"Good morning," she said. "Today we have a special treat."

Stop | Think | Write

CONCLUSIONS

Who is standing with Mrs. Nelson?

_____

_____

_____

145

"These firefighters will talk to us about fire **safety**," said Mrs. Nelson. "They will teach us some rules. We will learn how to avoid fires. We will also learn what to do if there is a fire."

Randy was sad. He liked gym a lot. Now he would have to wait until next week.

Stop **Think** **Write**

Randy's class is going to learn about fire

_____.

Ingrid came over. She was Randy's **buddy.** "What's wrong?" Ingrid said.

"Why do we have to learn about fire safety?" Randy said. "That's no fun."

"It may not be fun," she said. "Still, it's good to know."

"Maybe," he said. "I wanted to do tumbling today."

Stop | Think | Write

CAUSE AND EFFECT

Why is Randy sad?

_____

_____

_____

147

"Good morning," Chief Sims said. "We want you to be safe. The best rule is to avoid fires. Don't play with matches. They start fires."

Officer Jones gave a **speech** about smoke alarms. "Every house needs a smoke alarm," she said. "They save lives."

| Stop | Think | Write |

Officer Jones talks to the class. Her _____ is about smoke alarms.

"Now let's learn what to do if your clothes catch on fire," said Officer Jones. She pulled out the gray mats. "First, stop moving. Then drop to the floor. Then roll back and forth. Who wants to try?"

Randy tried "stop, drop, and roll." It was just like tumbling!

Stop **Think** **Write**

STORY STRUCTURE

Randy gets to roll on the

_____.

At recess, Ingrid played with Randy. "We learned a lot about fire safety today," she said.

"I learned something else," said Randy.

"What's that?" Ingrid asked.

"It was more fun than I thought!" he said.

Stop | Think | Write

UNDERSTANDING CHARACTERS

Randy has _____ learning about fire safety.

Look Back and Respond

1 Why is Randy disappointed after he gets to school?

Hint
See pages 146 and 147.

_____

_____

_____

2 Why should every house have a smoke alarm?

Hint
See page 148.

_____

_____

_____

3 What changes Randy's mind about fire safety?

Hint
See pages 149 and 150.

_____

_____

_____

Helping People

1 Helping a friend can be fun. You won't be **disappointed** if you help a friend.

Why won't you be <u>disappointed</u> if you work hard at school?

_____

_____

_____

2 I like to help people. I helped my brother learn to ride a bike. I was happy when he learned. He was, too. We both **chuckled**.

What is another word for <u>chuckled</u>?

_____

3 One day, I saw a girl at school. She was **staring** at the room numbers. I asked her if she needed help. She did. I showed her the right room.

Tell about a time you were <u>staring</u> at something unusual.

_____

_____

_____

4 Last Monday, I **received** a box. I looked at the name. The box was sent to the wrong house! I took it to Mr. Tam's house. He thanked me.

Tell about a time you <u>received</u> something in the mail.

_____

_____

_____

Kate's Helping Day

by Margaret Maugenest

Kate woke up early. It was a special day. She planned to help people.

Kate had promised to help her mom first. Kate was **staring** into space when her mom called her.

Stop **Think** **Write**

VOCABULARY

A word that has the same meaning as <u>staring</u> is

_____.

154

Kate's mom was wearing a hat and gloves. "Are you really going to help me?" asked Mom.

"Sure," said Kate. "May I wear a hat and gloves, too?"

"Yes," said Mom.

Stop **Think** **Write**

Kate wants to wear a hat and

_____ .

Kate helped out in the garden. Mom told her all about plants. Kate had fun.

"We've worked a long time. We're done, Kate," said Mom. "Who will you help next?"

STORY STRUCTURE

Kate helps her mom. She learns about

_____ .

"I'm helping my friend Carol," said Kate. "We're going to paint her room."

Kate put on some old clothes. Then she walked to Carol's home.

Kate hoped she'd like painting. It was hard but fun. She was not **disappointed**.

Stop **Think** **Write**

SEQUENCE OF EVENTS

Kate puts on old clothes. What does she do next?

_____

_____

_____

157

The friends liked painting the walls.
Paint splashed on their old clothes.
They looked in a mirror. They
chuckled about the paint spills.

VOCABULARY

Kate and Carol _____ about
the paint on their clothes.

Next, Kate helped her friend Ramón. She went to his house. They washed his dad's car.

It was hard work. It was worth it. Ramón's dad paid them. Each of them **received** a few dollars.

| Stop | Think | Write |

STORY STRUCTURE

Kate is at _____ house.

That night, Kate was tired but happy.
She thought about the day.

She had learned about plants.
She had made a room pretty. She had earned money.

Kate smiled. She liked helping out.

Stop **Think** **Write**

STORY STRUCTURE

At the end of the story, Kate feels tired and

_____ .

Look Back and Respond

1 What is Kate thinking about when the story begins?

Hint
For a clue, see page 154.

_____

_____

_____

2 Who does Kate help in the story?

Hint
There are clues on every page!

_____

_____

_____

3 Where does Kate go to help those people?

Hint
For clues, see pages 156, 157, and 159.

_____

_____

_____

A Good Teacher

Check the answer.

1 It was the _____ day of first grade. Lisa was sad. Now she had to say goodbye to Mr. Lee.

☐ busy ☐ final ☐ deepest

2 She thought about her year at school. Math was hard. Mr. Lee spent _____ time with her. He wanted to make sure she learned.

☐ extra ☐ rotten ☐ plain

3 It worked! Lisa did a fine job in math. She got a good test score. Mr. Lee _____ for her. She would miss Mr. Lee.

☐ hurried ☐ received ☐ cheered

4 What is the <u>final</u> thing you do before going to bed?

_____

_____

_____

5 Tell about a time you <u>hurried</u> somewhere.

_____

_____

_____

True Heroes

by Karen Bischoff

Josh loved baseball. The Stars were his favorite team. The player Rick Callan was his hero. Josh had never been to a game. He had seen games only on TV.

Stop   Think   Write

Josh's favorite baseball team is

_____ .

164

One day, Josh's dad came home smiling. "My boss had **extra** tickets to the game," he said. "He gave them to me." "Wow!" shouted Josh. He was happy.

Stop | Think | Write

SEQUENCE OF EVENTS

Josh's dad shows Josh tickets to the game. Then

Josh is _____.

165

The game was great. Josh could see all the players. He **cheered** a lot.

He loved to watch Rick Callan. He played like a hero. He hit a home run. The **final** score was 7 to 4. The Stars won.

VOCABULARY

The score at the end of the game is the

_____ score.

166

On the way to the car, Josh stopped. He saw Rick Callan! Josh **hurried** over to him. "Will you sign my program?" he asked.

"Sorry. I'm in a rush," Rick Callan said. He kept walking.

Stop | **Think** | **Write**

Josh _____ over to Rick Callan because he did not want to miss him.

Josh was upset. Rick Callan had not been nice to him. Josh said, "I thought he was a hero. I was wrong."

"Never mind," Dad said. "I can take you to a real hero."

SEQUENCE OF EVENTS

After meeting Rick Callan, Josh is

_____.

Josh's dad took him to a house. "Josh, this is Mrs. Evans. I had a secret. She helped me with it," Dad said.

"What was the secret?" Josh asked.

"I couldn't read," said Dad.

Stop | **Think** | **Write**

SEQUENCE OF EVENTS

Josh meets Mrs. Evans _____
the game.

"Mrs. Evans taught me to read," Dad said. "She's my hero. A hero teaches you something."

"Your dad is my hero," said Mrs. Evans. "He worked hard to learn."

Josh smiled. "I have two new heroes now," he said.

Stop **Think** **Write**

Josh's dad thinks Mrs. Evans is a

_____.

Look Back and Respond

1 Who is Josh's hero at the beginning of the story?

Hint
For a clue, see page 164.

_____

_____

_____

2 When does Josh meet Rick Callan?

Hint
For clues, see pages 166 and 167.

_____

_____

_____

3 Who are Josh's heroes at the end of the story?

Hint
For a clue, see page 170.

_____

_____

_____

How Writers Work

1 A writer uses words. The words explain how the writer feels. Words **express** the writer's feelings.

Do you write about your feelings? Name a feeling you might want to express.

2 Most writers say that they like to read. They say that reading books **taught** them to write.

Name something that books have taught you.

3 Writers use their imaginations. They may **pretend** they have done something. They may write about an event as if it really happened.

Do you ever <u>pretend</u> to be in a place that isn't real? Explain.

_____

_____

_____

4 Sometimes a very good book wins a **prize**.

Think of the books you like. What book would you give a <u>prize</u> to?

_____

_____

_____

Pat Mora

by Jean Casella

Pat Mora grew up in Texas.
She spoke two languages.
Pat spoke English. She spoke
Spanish, too.

Stop Think Write

MAIN IDEAS AND DETAILS

Pat spoke English and _____.

Pat's grandparents grew up in Mexico. Pat spoke Spanish with them.

Pat's aunt grew up in Mexico, too. She told stories about growing up there. She told some stories in English. She told some in Spanish. Pat loved her aunt's stories.

Stop **Think** **Write**

CAUSE AND EFFECT

Why did Pat's aunt speak Spanish?

_____

_____

_____

Pat loved to read. She read about places far away. She liked to **pretend** she was there.

There were always books in Pat's house. Her mother would drive her to the library, too.

Stop Think Write

Pat liked to _____ she was in a faraway place.

At school, all the lessons were in English. So Pat spoke English at school. She also spoke it at home.

When Pat grew up, she became a teacher. She **taught** kids to read and write.

Stop **Think** **Write**

VOCABULARY

Name the things Pat taught her students.

_____

_____

_____

177

Pat had a lot of ideas. She wanted to
write books. She wanted to **express** her
ideas in words.

Pat wanted to write about growing
up in Texas. She wanted to write
about speaking two languages.

Stop | **Think** | **Write**

UNDERSTANDING CHARACTERS

Why did Pat want to write books?

_____

_____

_____

178

Pat started to write books. Her books won a **prize**. Then she wrote more books.

Pat wrote about families like hers. She told stories, just like her aunt did.

Stop | **Think** | **Write**

UNDERSTANDING CHARACTERS

Why was Pat's aunt important to her?

_____

_____

_____

Some of Pat's books are in English. Some of her books are in Spanish.

Some of her books have English words and Spanish words. They use two languages—just like Pat!

MAIN IDEAS AND DETAILS

What is unusual about some of Pat's books?

_____

_____

_____

Look Back and Respond

1 **Where did Pat's family live?**

Hint

For a clue, see page 174.

_____

_____

_____

2 **Why did Pat want to write books?**

Hint

For clues, see page 178.

_____

_____

_____

3 **How was Pat like her aunt?**

Hint

For a clue, see page 179.

_____

_____

_____

agreed

failed

polite

trouble

A Wrong Turn

1️⃣ My sister and I had **trouble** finding our way. We took a wrong turn. We got lost.

Name something that you have <u>trouble</u> doing.

_____

_____

_____

2️⃣ We **failed** to get home. Our parents would be worried.

What was the last thing you <u>failed</u> to do?

_____

_____

_____

3 I said we should stop. We should ask for directions. My sister **agreed**.

What is something that you and your friends <u>agreed</u> on last week?

_____

_____

_____

4 A girl helped us. She told us how to get home. She was very **polite**.

Describe a way that you are <u>polite</u>.

_____

_____

_____

The Big City

by John Berry

Sam looked out the window. Texas was fading away. His dad was reading a paper. His mom was reading a book.

Sam's family was moving to New York City. Sam was sad. He missed Texas already.

Stop Think Write

Who is the author of this story?

_____

_____

_____

At last the plane landed. New York City looked very tall. Sam stared. He did not know this city. He did not have friends here. He might have **trouble** feeling at home.

Stop Think Write

UNDERSTANDING CHARACTERS

Sam doesn't know the city. He doesn't have any

_____ in New York.

They went to their new home. Sam couldn't sleep that night. He heard horns. He heard sirens. His mom and dad were awake, too.

"What shall we do tomorrow?" said his mom. "Let's plan."

Stop Think Write

TEXT AND GRAPHIC FEATURES

Sam and his dad look at the map to

_____ their day.

The next day, they got on the subway. Sam's dad wanted to go to a hardware store. They **failed** to get there. They were on the wrong subway. "Next stop, Yankee Stadium," said a voice.

"The baseball stadium?" said Sam. "Wow!"

Stop Think Write

VOCABULARY

The family took the wrong subway. They

_____ to get to the store.

Sam's mom and dad looked at him.
They looked at each other. They smiled.

"Shall we go to the game?" asked
his mom.

"Yes!" said Sam.

His dad **agreed**. They bought tickets.
It was a great game. It was a great day.

They took a subway the next day, too. Sam's mom wanted to shop for curtains. They got on the wrong subway again.

They looked at the map. A **polite** man helped. "Are you new here?" he said. "You're near a good museum. You should go there."

Stop Think Write

MAIN IDEAS AND DETAILS

The family is near a _____.

Sam and his family found the museum. They saw a blue whale. They saw rocks and gems. They saw bugs and snakes.

They walked into a big room. Sam stared. Dinosaurs! "Wow," said Sam. "New York isn't so bad after all!"

Stop **Think** **Write**

What is the family looking at?

_____

_____

_____

Look Back and Respond

1 Why can't Sam sleep during his first night in New York?

Hint
For a clue, see page 186.

_____

_____

_____

2 How does Sam's opinion of New York change?

Hint
For clues, see pages 185, 188, and 190.

_____

_____

_____

3 Is "The Big City" a good title for the story? Explain.

Hint
There are clues on almost every page!

_____

_____

_____

Lesson

20

✓ **TARGET VOCABULARY**

gazing

sore

sprang

studied

A Maple Tree

1 A girl was _____ at a tree. She thought it was pretty.

2 She knew it was a maple tree. She _____ trees in class. She knew the different types.

3 A gust of wind blew leaves off the

tree. She _____ up
and grabbed a rake.

4 Raking leaves was hard work. It

made her _____.
Her arms hurt.

**Write the vocabulary word that best
completes the synonym web.**

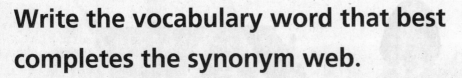

5   When you are _____
at something, you are

looking at it.   staring at it.   watching it.

Sue and the Tired Wolf

by John Berry

Sue lived in a blue house with her mom and dad. The house had a big yard. It was next to a forest.

Sue **studied** music. She played songs on her flute every day.

Stop **Think** **Write**

MAIN IDEAS AND DETAILS

Sue's house is next to a _____.

One day, Sue's mom and dad wanted some quiet. "Too much noise!" they said.

"I will go outside, then," said Sue. Her mom told her to play in the yard. She should not go in the woods. Sue agreed.

She sat in a leaf pile. She played her flute loudly.

Stop | **Think** | **Write**

Sue's mom and dad want less

_____ .

Sue got bored. She wanted to explore the woods. She told herself she would go for just a bit. She walked into the forest. The trees were tall. The forest was dark. Sue kept playing her flute. She liked the sound of her flute in the forest.

CAUSE AND EFFECT

Why does Sue walk into the forest?

_____

_____

_____

All of a sudden, Sue stopped playing. A wolf was sitting on a rock. He was **gazing** at her.

"You surprised me!" Sue said. She was scared. She tried to smile.

"I like the sound of your flute. I think this forest is too quiet," said the wolf.

Stop **Think** **Write**

UNDERSTANDING CHARACTERS

The wolf likes Sue's music. He thinks the

forest is too _____.

The wolf was tired and **sore**. He said, "I have been hunting all day. I want to rest and listen to music."

Sue played her flute. The wolf grew sleepy. His eyelids closed as Sue played.

VOCABULARY

The wolf has been hunting all day. His muscles

hurt. He is _____.

Sue began to run away, but the wolf woke up. He **sprang** off the rock. "Why did you stop?" he asked.

"I have to get home," said Sue.

"You can't go! Play more!"

Stop **Think** **Write**

The wolf woke up. Then he

_____ off the rock.

Sue blew a new tune. The wolf grew sleepy again. He started to snore.

Sue walked a few steps. Then she played again. The wolf snored louder. The trick seemed to work!

She used the trick a few more times. At last she was home! Now she knew why she had to stay out of the woods.

Stop Think Write

STORY STRUCTURE

How does Sue get away from the wolf?

_____

_____

_____

Look Back and Respond

1 Sue's yard is safe to play in. What is the forest like?

Hint
For clues, see pages 196 and 197.

_____

_____

2 What does the wolf think of Sue's music?

Hint
For a clue, see page 197.

_____

_____

3 Do you think Sue will go back to the forest?

Hint
For a clue, see page 200.

_____

_____

_____

Turtles

All turtles have shells. A turtle has a shell on the top. It has a shell on the bottom. The shells get **slippery** when they are wet.

A turtle needs its shell. The shell keeps the turtle safe. **Otherwise**, the turtle might get eaten. It has enemies!

Many turtles live in water. They have **webbed** feet. Water turtles sleep all winter. They sleep at the bottom of ponds and lakes. Then the spring comes. The water gets warm. **Finally**, the turtles wake up.

1. At the end of winter, the turtles

    _____ wake up.

2. A turtle's shell gets

    _____ when it is wet.

3. A turtle's shell keeps it safe.

    The turtle might be eaten,

    _____.

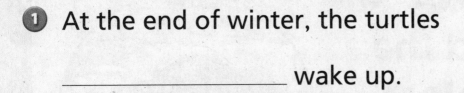

4. Name other animals that

    have <u>webbed</u> feet.

    _____

    _____

    _____

Joe and Trig
and the Baby Turtles

by Karen Bischoff

A turtle came out of a lake. She found some sand and made a nest with her **webbed** feet. Then she laid her eggs. The turtle pushed sand on top of her eggs. When her work was **finally** done, she went back to the lake.

Stop Think Write

The turtle has feet that are _____.

Many days passed. The eggs cracked. One baby turtle was fast. It got out of its shell first. It pushed its way out of the nest. It needed to get to the water. It was not safe on the ground. Birds like to eat baby turtles.

Stop **Think** **Write**

CAUSE AND EFFECT

Why does the turtle need to get to the water?

_____

_____

_____

Close by, Joe was fishing. His Uncle Rob brought him to the lake. Joe had his dog, Trig.

Trig was sniffing around the edge of the lake. Trig barked. Joe went over to Trig.

Stop Think Write

CONCLUSIONS

What makes Joe go to see Trig?

Trig had found the baby turtle. It was stuck in some mud.

"Good job, Trig!" said Joe.

Joe picked up the turtle. He put it in a pool of water near the lake. The turtle splashed up and down in the fresh water.

Stop **Think** **Write**

CAUSE AND EFFECT

Why does Joe pick up the baby turtle?

_____

_____

_____

Joe looked around. "Are there more turtles?" he asked Trig. "We may need to help them, too."

Trig sniffed the ground and tracked the baby turtle's path. Joe followed. They headed for the turtles' nest.

Stop | Think | Write

MAIN IDEAS AND DETAILS

Trig sniffed the path that led to the turtles'

_____.

Uncle Rob looked for Joe and Trig. "Where are you?" he called.

"We're over here," said Joe. "We're watching turtles."

Uncle Rob found them by the nest. The turtles were working hard. They had to dig their way out of the **slippery** sand.

Stop **Think** **Write**

VOCABULARY

It was hard for the turtles to get out of the nest because it was _____.

Joe and Uncle Rob watched the turtles go to the lake.

"They will be safe now," said Joe.

"It's good that you found that first turtle," said Uncle Rob. "Otherwise, they all might have been in trouble."

"Trig found it!" said Joe.

Stop **Think** **Write**

MAIN IDEAS AND DETAILS

Who found the first baby turtle?

_____

_____

_____

Look Back and Respond

1 **What is this story mostly about?**

_____

_____

_____

Hint

For a clue, read every page.

2 **Why were the turtle eggs in the sand?**

_____

_____

_____

Hint

For a clue, see page 204.

3 **What might have happened if Trig had not found the turtle?**

_____

_____

_____

Hint

For a clue, see page 205.

answered

heavily

planning

seriously

New Neighbors

① Dad helped people next door. He lugged big boxes. He was breathing **heavily**.

Why does Dad breathe heavily when he carries the boxes?

_____

_____

_____

② Dad spoke **seriously** to me. He asked me to go next door. He wanted me to introduce myself. **What do you do seriously?**

_____

_____

_____

3 I had chores to do. I was **planning** to take out the trash. Dad said it could wait.

What are you planning to do after school today?

_____

_____

_____

4 I rang my new neighbor's bell. A boy my age **answered**. Now I have a new friend!

Have you answered the phone recently? Who was calling?

_____

_____

_____

Flood on River Road

by Shirley Granahan

It rained all day. It rained all night.
It rained **heavily** for days.

"I am sick of rain," said Jody.

"Me, too," I said. "At least we're
warm and dry."

Stop **Think** **Write**

VOCABULARY

A lot of rain falls. It falls _____

for days.

214

We looked down the hill. Water covered River Road. It spilled into Mr. Lee's house.

"This is a flood!" Mom said **seriously**. "We must help Mr. Lee!"

Stop | **Think** | **Write**

UNDERSTANDING CHARACTERS

Mom wants to help _____.

Mr. Lee stayed at our house. He kept **planning** to go home. He had to wait until the water went down. At last, it did.

Mr. Lee went to his house. His things were wet and muddy. Neighbors gave him some new things to use.

Stop Think Write

What is Mr. Lee's house like after the flood?

_____

_____

_____

"Thank you!" he said. He was still worried. What if the water came back? "Can we have a party to make Mr. Lee happy again?" I asked Mom. "Good idea!" she **answered**.

Stop **Think** **Write**

VOCABULARY

What word could you use instead of <u>answered</u>?

_____

At the party, Jody and I sang a silly song. I barked like a dog.

There was a knock at the door. A man gave Mr. Lee a letter. He read it and smiled.

UNDERSTANDING CHARACTERS

Mr. Lee is _____ when he reads

the letter.

Mr. Lee showed us the letter. "I have been offered a new home," he said. "It is up on a hill. I will not have to worry about floods!"

Stop **Think** **Write**

UNDERSTANDING CHARACTERS

How does Mr. Lee feel about his new home?

_____

_____

_____

219

We were glad. The house was not far away. Mr. Lee would still be our neighbor!

"Come visit me," he said. "You, too, silly dog. You helped me to laugh!"

Stop | Think | Write

STORY STRUCTURE

People are glad that Mr. Lee will still be their

_____.

1 Is Mom a good neighbor? Explain.

Hint

For a clue, see page 215.

_____

_____

_____

2 How do Mr. Lee's neighbors help him after the flood?

Hint

For clues, see pages 216 and 217.

_____

_____

_____

3 How do you think Mr. Lee feels about his neighbors?

Hint

For clues, see pages 217 and 220.

_____

_____

_____

✓ **TARGET VOCABULARY**

duplicated

dye

strands

yarn

Making Things

1 Yolanda wants to make mittens. She needs to get **yarn** first.

Name something else you can knit with yarn.

_____

_____

_____

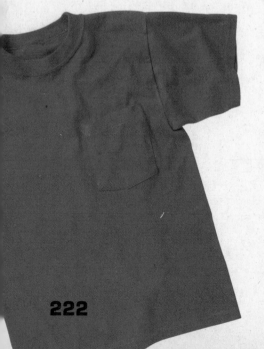

2 Tim has a white shirt. He soaks it in red **dye**. Now he has a red shirt.

You soaked a white shirt in blue dye. What color is the shirt now?

_____

_____

_____

3 Javier has **strands** of yarn. They are red, blue, and white. He braids the yarn. He makes a bracelet.

You want to make a friendship bracelet from <u>strands</u> of yarn. Which colors would you pick?

_____

_____

_____

4 Nick made a drawing. Nora wants to make one like it. She copies the drawing. Hers looks just the same! She **duplicated** his drawing.

What have you <u>duplicated</u>?

_____

_____

_____

I Made It Myself

by Margaret Maugenest

My grandma and I take a walk. We pass a shop window. I point to a red scarf.

"That's pretty," I say.

"You can knit a scarf like this," says Ama. "I'll show you how, Rosie."

"Really?" I ask.

Stop **Think** **Write**

Rosie likes a red

_____.

We go to Ama's house. Ama gets a box. Inside are balls of white **yarn**.

"You can use this to make a scarf," she says.

"This yarn is white," I say. "I want a red scarf."

Stop **Think** **Write**

To knit, you need balls of

_____

"I can make it red," says Ama. "I know how. I'll soak it in red **dye**."

"You're so smart. You can do anything!" I say. I give Ama a big hug.

I go to Ama's house the next day. The wool is red.

UNDERSTANDING CHARACTERS

Rosie thinks Ama is

_____.

"Let's knit," Ama says.

She shows me how to hold the knitting needles. "Bring the yarn under first. Then bring it over the needle," she says.

Stop **Think** **Write**

MAIN IDEAS AND DETAILS

Ama shows Rosie how to

_____.

I make my first stitch.
I make another stitch.
I finish my first row.
Then I knit another row.

"I don't see much
scarf yet," I say.

"It takes time,"
says Ama.

"It sure does!" I say.

CONCLUSIONS

It takes a lot of

_____ **to knit.**

I knit every day. My cat Ruby likes to watch. I cut some **strands** of yarn. She plays with them.

My scarf starts to get long.

I keep knitting. My scarf is getting longer!

Stop **Think** **Write**

CONCLUSIONS

How can you tell Rosie likes to knit?

_____

_____

_____

I knit for many weeks.

At last, my scarf is done. Ama helps me finish it. I put it around my neck.

"Thank you. It is beautiful," I say.

"I'm proud of you," says Ama. "You **duplicated** the scarf! You're a real knitter!"

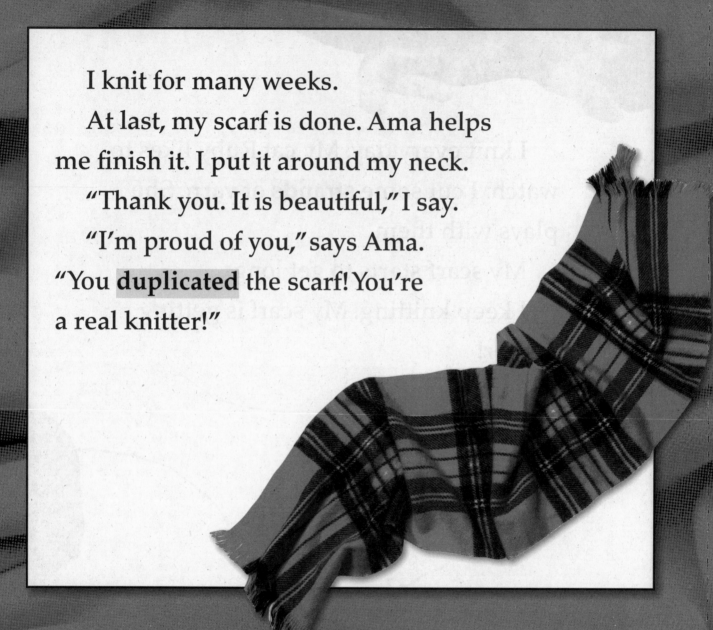

Stop **Think** **Write**

VOCABULARY

Rosie is a real knitter. She

_____ the red scarf she saw.

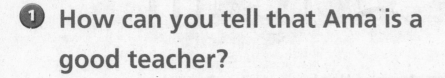

Look Back and Respond

1 How can you tell that Ama is a good teacher?

Hint

For clues, see pages 227 and 228.

_____

_____

_____

2 Does it take Rosie a long time to knit her scarf? How do you know?

Hint

For clues, see pages 228, 229, and 230.

_____

_____

_____

3 How can you tell that Rosie and Ama get along well?

Hint

Clues are on almost every page!

_____

_____

_____

By the Stream

I took my little paper boat
And put it in the **stream**.
The boat was bobbing up and down.
I fell into a dream.

I sailed the mighty Rio Grande.
For Big Bend, I was bound.
The rushing water got quite **swift**.
The boat was **flung** around.

I dreamed it ran into a rock
And sank into the deep.
But all was well, and so I fell
Back **peacefully** to sleep.

1. The boat was _____
   this way and that in the water.

2. I put my paper boat into the
   _____.

3. The rushing water became very
   _____.

4. Describe a place where you can sit
   peacefully.

   _____

   _____

   _____

The Contest

by Mia Lewis

Sun and Wind were talking.

"I'm stronger than you," said Wind.
"I can blow a ship across the sea. I can bend a tree to the ground."

"I'm stronger!" said Sun. "I light the day. I can dry up that **stream**!"

Stop **Think** **Write**

VOCABULARY

If you walk in a _____, your feet will get wet.

Sun saw a man on the road.

"That man is wearing a coat," said Sun. "We will have a contest. If you can make the man take off his coat, you are stronger. If I can make him take it off, I am stronger. You go first!"

Stop **Think** **Write**

CAUSE AND EFFECT

Why does Sun want to have a contest?

_____

_____

_____

_____

Wind agreed. He wasted no time. He blew a **swift** breeze at the man. The traveler did not notice.

Wind blew a stronger gust. The man held onto his hat. He kept walking.

CAUSE AND EFFECT

Why does Wind blow a strong gust at the man?

_____

_____

_____

Now Wind blew a real storm! The trees shook! Leaves were **flung** into the air.

Wind blew as hard as he could. The man only pulled his coat more tightly around himself.

Stop · Think · Write

VOCABULARY

The strong wind _____ the leaves into the air.

At last Wind gave up. "You try," he said to Sun. "Good luck!"

Sun smiled. He shone a little ray. The man kept on walking.

"You see," said Wind. "Neither of us can get him to take off his coat."

Stop | Think | Write

Why do you think Sun smiles?

Sun was not finished. He shone another ray on the man. He beat down hot and steady.

The man began to sweat. He took off his hat. He opened his coat. After a while, he took his coat all the way off.

Stop **Think** **Write**

CAUSE AND EFFECT

Why does the man take off his coat ?

_____

_____

_____

Wind clapped. Sun bowed. The man walked **peacefully** down the road in his T-shirt.

The story has a moral. Persuade gently. It works better than force.

Stop | Think | Write

Why does Sun bow?

_____

_____

_____

Look Back and Respond

1 Why does the man pull his coat around him tightly?

Hint

For a clue, see page 237.

_____

_____

_____

2 Why does the man remove his hat?

Hint

For a clue, see page 239.

_____

_____

_____

3 Write the moral of the story in your own words.

Hint

Read the moral on page 240.

_____

_____

_____

How Flowers Grow

**blossomed
drooping
sprouting
underneath**

1 Some flowers begin as seeds. A seed is planted in the spring. The seed is placed **underneath** the surface of the soil.

Write a word that has the same meaning as <u>underneath</u>.

_____

2 Spring comes. The soil warms up. The seed is now **sprouting**. The plant begins to grow! Soon it will be a flower.

Name a place you might find a seed that is <u>sprouting</u>.

_____

_____

_____

3 This flower has **blossomed**. The flower grows on a stem. The stem gets water from the roots.

Name a plant you have seen that has <u>blossomed</u>.

_____

_____

_____

4 After the flower blooms, it begins **drooping**. Then it dries out.

Write a word that tells what a flower is like when it is <u>drooping</u>.

_____

_____

_____

Daffodils

by Claire Daniel

It is spring! Look at the flowers. Many have **blossomed**. They tell us, "Nice days are here again!"

Daffodils are one of the first flowers of spring. They grow in bunches.

Stop | **Think** | **Write**

MAIN IDEAS AND DETAILS

_____ are one of the first flowers of spring.

Daffodils can grow two ways. They can grow from seeds. They can grow from bulbs.

Bulbs are **underneath** the surface of the ground. They store food for the plant. New daffodils grow from bulbs.

Stop | Think | Write

VOCABULARY

The bulbs are _____ the ground.

In winter, the bulb stays in the ground. The bulb stores food. The daffodil will use the food in the spring.

Spring is here! A small green shoot is **sprouting**. Roots grow down into the soil.

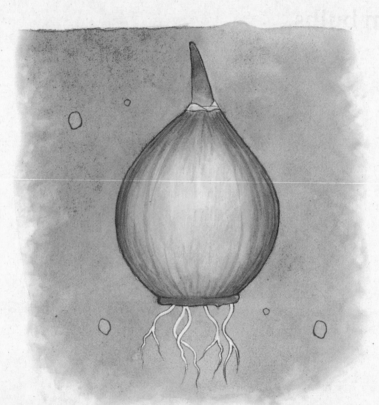

Stop   Think   Write

SEQUENCE OF EVENTS

In the spring, a small green _____ begins to grow.

The shoot becomes leaves. The leaves grow taller. They use energy from the sun to make food.

The roots are busy, too. They take in water. The plant needs water to grow.

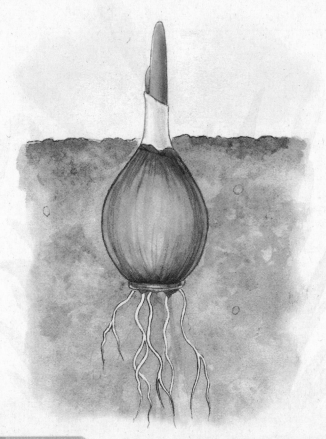

Stop   Think   Write

MAIN IDEAS AND DETAILS

The daffodil leaves grow taller. At the same

time, the roots take in _____.

A stem grows from the bulb. It grows taller and taller. A bud is on the end of the stem. The bud gets bigger. Then it blooms. The flower will last for weeks.

SEQUENCE OF EVENTS

The stem grows taller and taller. Then the bud _____.

Later, the flowers fall off. The **drooping** leaves turn brown. Then they dry up.

The bulb stays alive. It stores food for the plant. Next spring, the daffodil will bloom again!

Stop **Think** **Write**

VOCABULARY

The flowers fall off. Then the _____ leaves turn brown.

Daffodils make seeds. When the flower falls, the seeds fall, too. It can take years for the seeds to grow into daffodils.

Each spring, more daffodils bloom. They bring a sunny end to winter!

Seeds

MAIN IDEAS AND DETAILS

Daffodils grow from bulbs and from _____.

Look Back and Respond

1 In spring, what parts of a new daffodil grow first?

Hint
For a clue, see page 246.

_____

_____

_____

2 A bud grows bigger and bigger. What happens next?

Hint
For a clue, see page 248.

_____

_____

_____

3 What part of the daffodil stays alive in the winter?

Hint
For a clue, see page 249.

_____

_____

_____

✓ **TARGET VOCABULARY**

confused

ordinary

sensible

training

What a Teacher Does

1 A teacher is not an **ordinary** person. It takes a special person to teach!

What do you do after school on an <u>ordinary</u> day?

_____

_____

_____

2 Teachers need to know a lot. People need **training** before they can teach.

Name someone else who needs <u>training</u>.

_____

_____

_____

252

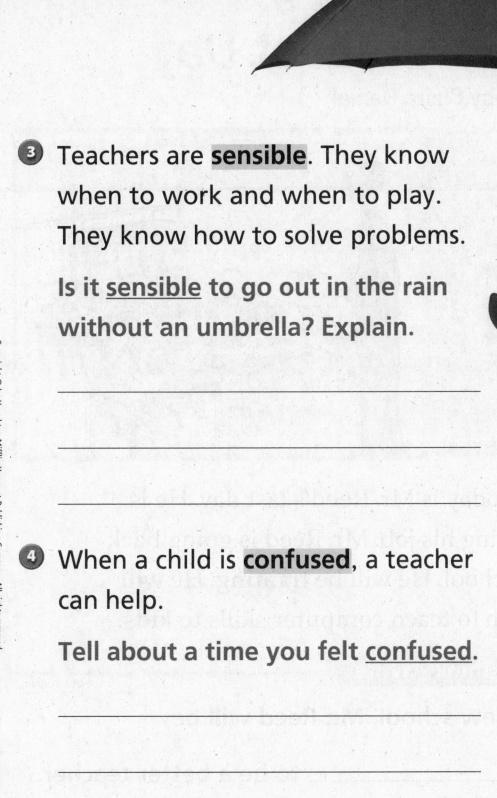

3 Teachers are **sensible**. They know when to work and when to play. They know how to solve problems.

Is it <u>sensible</u> to go out in the rain without an umbrella? Explain.

_____

_____

_____

4 When a child is **confused**, a teacher can help.

Tell about a time you felt <u>confused</u>.

_____

_____

_____

Mr. Reed's Last Day

by Claire Daniel

Today is Mr. Reed's last day. He is leaving his job. Mr. Reed is going back to school. He will be **training**. He will learn to teach computer skills to kids.

Stop Think Write

VOCABULARY

At his new school, Mr. Reed will be

_____ to be a better teacher.

It is his last day. His students know. They smile a lot. No one says a thing.

Mr. Reed wants to go learn more. It is a **sensible** thing to do. Still, he is not so happy. He is leaving. He thinks the children do not care.

Stop | **Think** | **Write**

UNDERSTANDING CHARACTERS

Why isn't Mr. Reed happy?

_____

_____

_____

The principal comes to class. She
brings Curt and Gina. They wink at each
other.

"Now I need Ann," the principal says.
"Her father is here."

"This is odd," Mr. Reed says. The
children just smile.

All day long, the principal picks up children. Then she brings them back.

Mr. Reed gives the children a test. They do not mind. They smile and smile. Mr. Reed says, "That's odd, too."

Stop | **Think** | **Write**

STORY STRUCTURE

The principal picks up children and

_____ them back.

257

Then the principal asks for Ann, Gina, and Curt again. Now Mr. Reed is very **confused.**

Curt, Ann, and Gina come back. They have food, party hats, and a big box.

"Surprise!" the children yell.

Stop Think Write

VOCABULARY

Mr. Reed is _____ because so many children come and go.

Ann says, "My dad brought this balloon."

Gina says, "The principal helped us write notes."

Curt says, "We put the notes onto the balloon. They will make you think of us."

Stop Think Write

STORY STRUCTURE

All the children helped to make the

_____.

Now Mr. Reed is happy. He says, "This is no **ordinary** surprise!"

He ties the balloon to his bike. He rides home. The students wave. They will miss him.

Stop | Think | Write

STORY STRUCTURE

The surprise shows Mr. Reed that the children will _____ him.

Look Back and Respond

1 What is the problem in this story?

_____

_____

_____

Hint

For a clue, see page 255.

2 What do the children do on Mr. Reed's last day?

_____

_____

_____

Hint

For clues, see pages 258, 259, and 260.

3 How does this story end?

_____

_____

_____

Hint

Hint: For a clue, see page 260.

Different Kinds of Places

1 A boy dug in his yard. He had to

_____ some

rocks.

2 The boy _____

a tin box. It looked old.

3 A letter was in the box. He saw the date. It was long ago. Its

_____ date was

June 6, 1901.

4 The boy looked at the name. His great-grandma wrote the letter! The boy was

_____ !

Write the vocabulary word that best completes the synonym web.

5

When you are

_____ , you

are shocked.

say, "Wow!"

are surprised.

Discovering the Past

by John Berry

What was life like long ago? What did houses look like? What games did kids play? What did they eat?

The answers might be under your feet.

Stop **Think** **Write**

INFER AND PREDICT

What do you think this story will be about?

_____

_____

_____

264

Things were left in the dirt. Time passed. Then people **discovered** the things. People found old coins. They found toys. They found old tools.

These old things are clues. They tell us about the past.

Stop | Think | Write

Old things can tell us about _____.

Some people study the past. It's a fun job. They dig in the dirt.

They find old coins. They find pots. They find tools. These things tell a story. It's a story of the past.

FACT AND OPINION

The author says that studying the past is a fun job. Is that a fact or an opinion?

_____

_____

_____

266

The diggers make a map. The map shows the **exact** places where people find things.

A coin may be deep in the dirt. The map shows where. A pot may be next to a wall. The map shows where.

Stop | Think | Write

VOCABULARY

The map is correct. It shows the

_____ place where people found

things.

Scientists **remove** dirt. They study each item. They think about where it was found.

A toy was deep in the dirt. Another toy was near the top. The diggers may think the first toy is older.

Stop   Think   Write

VOCABULARY

Scientists clean the things that they find.

They _____ the dirt.

268

People learn from what they find.
They thought a pot was for water. It
looked like a water pot.

Then they looked closer. They found
oil inside the pot. They found bits of
food. They were **amazed**. The pot was for
cooking!

Stop **Think** **Write**

Look at the sentence: "The pot was for
cooking!" Is that a fact or an opinion?

_____

_____

_____

You don't have to dig. You can see old things at a museum. You can look at tools. You can look at coins. You can look at toys.

They will tell you about life long ago. Learning about the past is fun.

Stop Think Write

MAIN IDEA AND DETAILS

You can find old things in the dirt. You can also see old things in _____.

Look Back and Respond

1 Which sentence on page 270 is an opinion?

_____

_____

_____

Hint

Remember that you can agree or disagree with an opinion.

2 Sometimes scientists change their minds about old things. Why?

_____

_____

_____

Hint

See pages 268 and 269.

3 Do you think digging for old things would be a fun job? Explain.

_____

_____

_____

_____

Hint

Think about what diggers do and what they discover.

Lesson

28

✓ TARGET VOCABULARY

explored

force

orbit

space

A Long Trip

1 In 2003, a robot traveled through **space**. It was going to Mars.

Where in space would you like to visit?

_____

_____

_____

2 The robot had to **orbit** Mars. It circled the planet many times.

Explain what it means to orbit something.

_____

_____

_____

3 The robot landed in 2004. It **explored** Mars. It drove around. It tested the soil. It took pictures.

Name a place that you have explored.

_____

_____

_____

4 The robot had the **force** to drill into rocks.

What is something you need <u>force</u> to do?

_____

_____

_____

Apollo 11: The Eagle Has Landed

by John Berry

Three men sat in a rocket. They heard the countdown. 5, 4, 3, 2, 1.

The rocket roared into the sky. The **force** of the engines pushed the men back in their seats.

They were going to the Moon. It was July 16, 1969.

Stop | **Think** | **Write**

The men felt the _____ of the engines.

Into Space

The rocket went up and up. After 11 minutes, it began to **orbit** Earth. The rocket had to fly around Earth one and a half times.

Then its engines fired again. The men smiled. Earth was behind them. They were leaving.

Stop | **Think** | **Write**

VOCABULARY

The rocket flew around Earth. It had to

_____ **the planet.**

The men checked their tools. They rested. They looked out the window. **Space** was black and full of stars.

They reached the Moon in four days. Two of the men got into part of the rocket. This part was called the Eagle. It began to descend.

Stop Think Write

INFER AND PREDICT

Why do you think the men checked their tools?

On the Moon

"Houston," one man said, "The Eagle has landed." He opened the door.

The captain climbed down a ladder. He stepped onto the Moon. He was the first person to walk there.

Then he took a photo of the next man to touch the Moon.

Stop	Think	Write

TEXT AND GRAPHIC FEATURES

What does the photo show?

_____

_____

_____

Exploring the Moon

The men **explored**. They walked around. They collected rocks and dirt. They did tests. They took a lot of photos.

There is no rain on the Moon. There is no wind. A footprint can last many years.

Stop | Think | Write

CAUSE AND EFFECT

Why would a footprint last for years on the Moon?

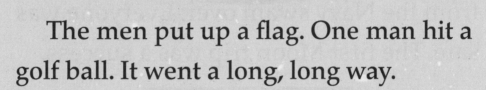

The men put up a flag. One man hit a golf ball. It went a long, long way.

They spent two hours on the Moon. Then they climbed the ladder. It was time to go. Engines fired. Up they went.

Soon they were back on the main rocket. They headed for Earth.

Stop | **Think** | **Write**

TEXT AND GRAPHIC FEATURES

What flag did the men leave on the Moon?

_____

_____

_____

Back to Earth

They looked out the window. Earth grew bigger. They were getting close to home.

The rocket splashed into the Pacific Ocean. The men got into a boat. A man from the Navy swam over. Everyone was safe. The first Moon trip was a success.

Why is this section called "Back to Earth"?

Look Back and Respond

1 Read the title. Why did the author choose this title?

Hint
For clues, see pages 276 and 277.

_____

_____

_____

2 What did the rocket do before heading to the Moon?

Hint
For a clue, see the section called "Into Space."

_____

_____

_____

3 Which ocean did the rocket land in?

Hint
For a clue, see the section called "Back to Earth."

_____

_____

_____

grateful

odd

search

startled

Cats

Cats are silent when they walk. They can sneak up on you. You might be **startled** when you see a cat.

Cats are happy when you pet them. They purr to show that they are **grateful**.

This is an **odd** fact. A cat meows to people. It doesn't make that sound to other animals.

You can find out more about cats. You can **search** the library for cat books.

1 Cats are _____ when you pet them.

2 You can _____ for books in the library.

3 It's an _____ fact that cats don't meow to other animals.

4 Tell about one time when you were <u>startled</u>. What happened?

_____

_____

_____

Fluff, Gus, and Bob

by Richard Stull

Fluff, Gus, and Bob lived together in a house. Fluff was an orange cat. Gus was gray. Bob was black and white.

Stop | **Think** | **Write**

The orange cat's name is _____.

"Let's **search** the cupboard," said Fluff. "We'll find something to eat there." Fluff ran to the cupboard. She found cans of cat food.

"We can't open the cans," said Gus and Bob.

Stop **Think** **Write**

VOCABULARY

Fluff wants to _____ in the cupboard for something to eat.

"I know what to do," said Fluff. "Let's ask Jimmy to help."

"Jimmy doesn't know we can talk," said Gus and Bob. "He might find it **odd** that cats can talk."

Stop **Think** **Write**

Which cat seems to make most decisions?

_____

Just then, Jimmy came home from school. First he petted the cats. Then he turned on the TV to watch cartoons.

Fluff, Gus, and Bob all spoke at once. "Hey, Jimmy," they said. "We want something to eat."

Stop | **Think** | **Write**

SEQUENCE OF EVENTS

What is the first thing Jimmy does when he gets home from school?

_____

_____

_____

287

Jimmy jumped up from his chair. "Who said that?" he asked.

"We did," said the cats. "We're sorry if we **startled** you."

"You see, we're hungry," said Fluff.

"We're starving," said Gus and Bob.

Stop **Think** **Write**

CAUSE AND EFFECT

Why is Jimmy surprised?

_____

_____

_____

"Cats can't talk!" said Jimmy.

"Of course we can talk," said Fluff.

"Do you think we just sleep all day?" asked Gus and Bob.

"Well," said Jimmy. "Now I know that you can talk."

UNDERSTANDING CHARACTERS

Which two cats always talk at the same time?

_____

_____

_____

"I'm glad you can talk," said Jimmy. "I've got three new friends."

"Three hungry friends," said the cats.

"Oh," said Jimmy. "I almost forgot." He opened a can of cat food for his **grateful** friends.

Stop Think Write

VOCABULARY

The cats are _____ for the food.

290

Look Back and Respond

1 **Why do the cats talk to Jimmy?**

Hint

For a clue, see page 287.

_____

_____

_____

2 **Fluff finds food in the cupboard. Why don't the cats eat it?**

Hint

For a clue, see page 285.

_____

_____

_____

3 **Jimmy is a kind person. How do you know?**

Hint

For clues, see pages 287 and 290.

_____

_____

_____

A Farm Invention

1 Eli Whitney **designed** the cotton gin. It cleaned seeds from cotton.

Name something that was designed a long time ago.

_____

_____

_____

2 Whitney worked hard. His first plans were not good. At last he made a plan that worked. He was able to **achieve** his goal.

What do you want to achieve?

_____

_____

_____

3 The cotton gin was a **remarkable** machine. It helped people work faster.

Name a **remarkable** machine in your house.

_____

_____

_____

4 Farmers liked the cotton gin. They needed fewer workers. The **result** was cheaper cotton.

What might be the **result** of studying hard for a test?

_____

_____

_____

Cyrus McCormick and His Reaper

by John Berry

A Boy Who Made Things

Cyrus McCormick was born in 1809. He lived on a farm. He liked to make things.

Cyrus had a dream. He wanted to be an inventor. He made a new tool when he was fifteen. He used it to carry grain.

Stop **Think** **Write**

UNDERSTANDING CHARACTERS

Cyrus dreamed of being an

_____.

294

A Good Idea

Farmers cut grain by hand. They used a big blade. It was hard work.

Cyrus's dad wanted to cut grain faster. He **designed** a machine. He made it. It never ran right.

Stop **Think** **Write**

MAIN IDEAS AND DETAILS

Farmers worked many hours to cut grain. Cyrus's dad wanted to make the work

_____ .

Cyrus's Reaper

Cyrus wanted to try. He made a new machine. It cut grain fast. It would help farmers cut more. It was called a reaper.

He worked on the machine for ten years. He wanted to make it better. He wanted to **achieve** his goal.

Stop **Think** **Write**

MAIN IDEAS AND DETAILS

Cyrus wanted to make the reaper better. He

worked on it for _____ years.

At last, Cyrus got a good **result**. The reaper worked better. It had an extra blade. It could cut grain in the rain.

Another man made a reaper. He wanted to have a contest. Whose reaper would work best?

Stop **Think** **Write**

VOCABULARY

The _____ of Cyrus's hard work was a better reaper.

Battle of the Reapers

The day of the contest was rainy. The other reaper jammed. Cyrus's reaper did not. It cut a lot of grain.

People wanted to buy Cyrus's reaper. He sold twenty-nine machines that year.

Stop **Think** **Write**

CONCLUSIONS

Cyrus was the _____ of the contest. His machine worked the best.

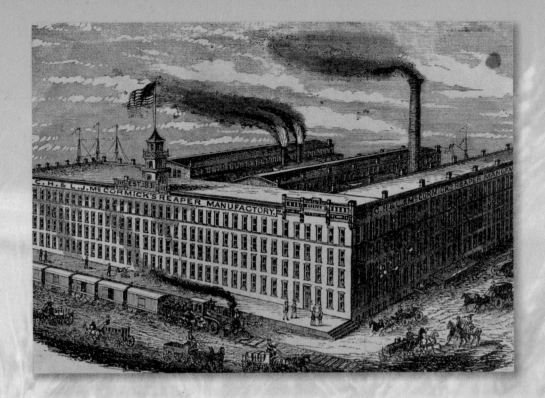

A New Place to Work

Cyrus made reapers on his farm. Many farmers wanted them. Cyrus needed more space.

He moved to Chicago. Workers in his factory made reapers fast. Cyrus sold thousands of machines each year.

Stop **Think** **Write**   COMPARE AND CONTRAST

Cyrus made more reapers at his

_____ than on his farm.

Success

The reaper was a success. Cyrus was famous all over the world.

He went to London in 1851. He got a medal for his work. His **remarkable** machine changed farming forever.

Stop   Think   Write

VOCABULARY

People thought the reaper was

_____.

Look Back and Respond

1 How did Cyrus's reaper change farm work?

Hint

For clues, see pages 296 and 297.

_____

_____

_____

2 How did Cyrus improve his machine?

Hint

For a clue, see page 297.

_____

_____

_____

3 Why did Cyrus move his work to a factory?

Hint

For a clue, see page 299.

_____

_____

_____

Summarize Strategy

You can **summarize** what you read.

- Tell important ideas in your own words.

- Tell ideas in an order that makes sense.

- Keep the meaning of the text.

- Use only a few sentences.

Analyze/Evaluate Strategy

You can **analyze** and **evaluate** a text. Think carefully about what you read. Form an opinion about it.

1. Think about the text and the author.

   - What are the important facts and ideas?

   - What does the author want you to know?

2. Decide what is important. Then form an opinion.

   - How do you feel about what you read?

   - Do you agree with the author's ideas?

Infer/Predict Strategy

Use clues to figure out what the author does not tell you. Then you are making an **inference**.

Use clues to figure out what will happen next. Then you are making a **prediction**.

Monitor/Clarify Strategy

Monitor what you read. Make sure it makes sense.

Find a way to understand what does not.

- Reread.

- Read ahead.

- Ask questions.

Question Strategy

Ask yourself **questions** as you read.

Look for answers.

Some questions to ask:

- What does the author mean?
- Who or what is this about?
- Why did this happen?
- What is the main idea?

Visualize Strategy

You can **visualize**.

- Make pictures in your mind as you read.
- Use words in the text to help you.
- Make pictures of people, places, things, and actions.

PHOTO CREDITS